Nursery Stitch

Nursery Stitch

20 Projects to Make

Rebecca Shreeve

COLLINS & BROWN

First published in the United
Kingdom by Collins & Brown
10 Southcombe Street
London W14 0RA

An imprint of
Anova Books Company Ltd

ISBN 978-1-84340-522-1

A CIP catalogue for this book is
available from the British Library.

10 9 8 7 6 5 4 3 2 1

Reproduction by Rival Colour Ltd, UK
Printed and bound by 1010 Printing
International Ltd, China.

This book can be ordered direct
from the publisher at
www.anovabooks.com.

contents

6 Introduction

9 Sheep T-Shirt

13 Cheeky Monkey Socks

17 Bunny Bib

21 Elephant Pillowcase

25 Whale Towel

29 Teddy Hat

33 Rabbit Blankie

39 Monster Play Mat

45 Doggy Draught Excluder

51 Kitten Cushion

55 Animal Textile Picture

59 Giant Piggy Cushion

63 Henry the Pig

69 Sleepy Ted Mobile

75 Toy Tidy

81 Ella the Mouse

87 Olivia the Sheep

93 Lucy the Elephant

99 Luke the Monkey

103 Animal Book

106 Techniques

introduction

Meet the menagerie! In this book you'll find a whole family of friendly animals waiting to share your child's day – from getting dressed to mealtimes, playtime, snoozetime, bathtime and bedtime. Whilst designing the projects, my aim has been to make original items that will not only be loved by children but cherished by their parents too. So often, toys and home textiles for children are brash and unsophisticated. I wanted to create a range of projects that are contemporary, yet quaint and quirky, and which will sit happily in a family home.

When it comes to selecting fabrics for the projects, it's vital to remember how delicate a baby's skin is. For garments and any home furnishings that are going to be next to the skin, such as pillow cases or comforters, use soft, natural fibres that allow the skin to breathe. Lightweight cottons (ideally organic), soft flannels and cotton fleeces are ideal. Avoid synthetic fabrics such as polyester and heavy wools that might scratch or irritate the skin. And, whatever you choose, make sure it's machine washable and quick drying. For toys, the choice of fabric is not so critical and you could use furnishing-weight cottons or even hard-wearing corduroy.

There's a bewildering choice of fabric patterns on the market, and my advice is to stick to simple patterns such as checks, spots, stripes or a simple repeat. I gather fabrics from many different places, as well as dedicated fabric shops for dressmaking and furnishing. Quilting stores sell 'fat quarters' in all kinds of wonderful patterns, which are ideal when you need only a small piece of material for an appliqué motif. Charity shops can be also a useful source of inexpensive cotton shirts and blouses, which you can then cut up and re-use.

Always wash your fabrics before you cut out the pieces and begin stitching. This minimizes the risk of shrinkage and allows you to check that the fabrics are colour fast.

Safety, of course, is paramount when it comes to making clothes and toys for babies. Little fingers have a surprisingly strong grip, and the constant gnawing and sucking of much-loved toys and comforters can loosen even the strongest stitching. So do not embellish your hand-made toys with buttons, beads, or anything else that could be pulled off and swallowed. Instead, add details with simple hand embroidery stitches.

Above all, when making toys, make sure that your seams are really firm and secure, so that no toy stuffing can come out. Work a few stitches in reverse at the start and end of each seam for security and, if seams intersect, check carefully to ensure that there are no gaps.

I feel I have put part of myself into every project; each item works well with the others, but every one is wonderfully unique. I hope you have as much fun making these projects as I did designing and creating them, and that they will be appreciated for years to come by their owners.

Rebecca Shreeve

sheep t-shirt

Baby's T-shirt (plain colour)

Scraps of patterned cotton fabric (body)

Scraps of neutral (plain or patterned) cotton fabric (face and legs)

Double-sided fusible webbing (such as Bondaweb)

Embroidery thread (black and various colours)

Embroidery needle

Erasable fabric marker or iron-on transfer pen (optional)

This T-shirt is for a two-year-old, but you can easily enlarge the sheep for any size of shirt. If you really love to sew, why not cover a whole T-shirt in sheep? The sheep would work perfectly on a tot's pyjamas – fun for counting yourself to sleep!

instructions

Transfer the templates to the webbing: place the webbing over a template, paper side up, and trace the lines of the template. Cut out the shape roughly.

Place each shape, paper side up, on the wrong side of the appropriate fabric. Iron for 3–4 seconds (no steam).

Cut out the shapes accurately. Peel off the backing paper and lay the body and legs, coated side down, on the right side of the T-shirt (use the photo for guidance on positioning). The legs of each sheep should be tucked under the body piece.

Iron in place (see page 107); if the T-shirt fabric is very thin, you may need to put greaseproof paper in the middle of the shirt as a precaution to prevent the glue from the webbing seeping through to the back of the shirt. Peel off the backing paper from

Please use at 100%   template

Cut the face, body and legs as separate pieces.

the sheep's face and position it on the body. Iron in place. Repeat for the other sheep and leave the motifs to cool.

horizontal stitches from one side of the leg to the other. (For details of how to work the hand stitches, see pages 108–11.)

Whipstitch around the head and body using three strands of embroidery thread and working over the edges of the motif and through the T-shirt. Make small stitches with a fairly small space between each one. Sew over each leg with a series of

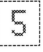

Sew on the facial features using three strands of embroidery thread and backstitch, making French knots for the eyes. If you prefer to have a drawn line to follow, use an erasable fabric marker or an iron-on transfer pen (see page 107).

cheeky monkey socks

Pair of baby's socks
(plain colour)

Scraps of patterned cotton
fabric (head and body)

Scraps of beige or cream
corduroy (face and
inner ear)

Double-sided fusible webbing
(such as Bondaweb)

Embroidery thread
(black and yellow, or
colour to suit)

Embroidery needle

Erasable fabric marker
or iron-on transfer pen
(optional)

These socks will certainly suit your cheeky little monkey. They would also make a fabulous present for a new baby, using more subtle colours such as pale blue or pink. Alternatively, for an older child, why not enlarge the monkey and put it on slippers?

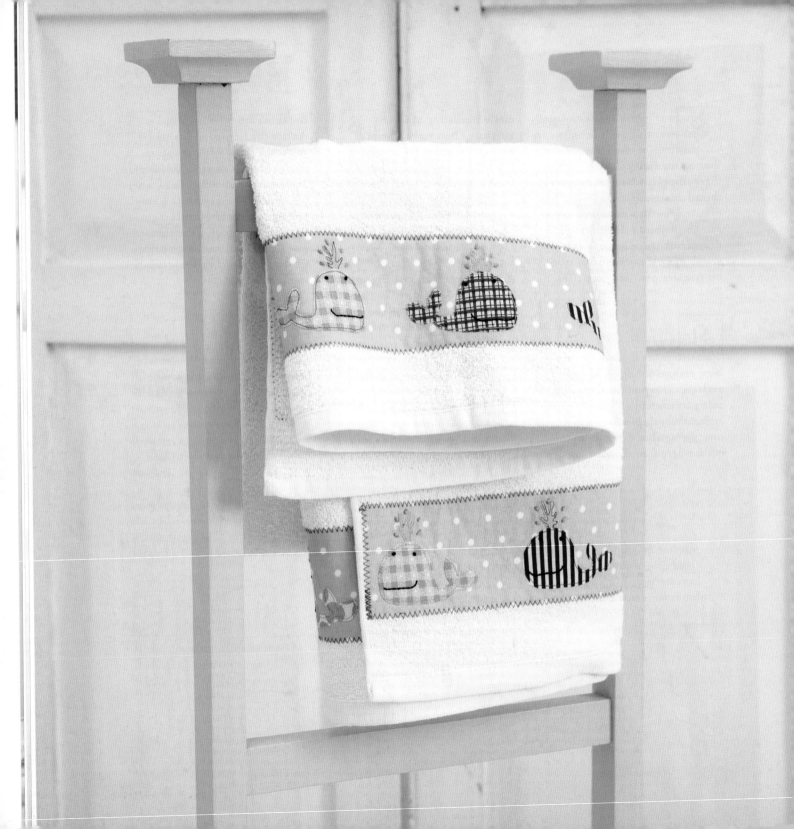

whale towel

Plain towel in a pale colour

Scraps of patterned cotton fabric (whales and water spurts)

Cotton fabric: a little wider than the width of towel x 25cm (10in) (sea background)

Double-sided fusible webbing (such as Bondaweb) (size as for sea background, plus sufficient to back whales)

Embroidery thread (black and blue)

Embroidery needle

Sewing machine with a freehand foot and a zigzag foot

Sewing thread

Erasable fabric marker

Ruler

Iron-on transfer pen (optional)

This very simple and satisfying project is a great way to jazz up a plain towel – and it will make bathtime more fun. You can adjust the pattern for a bigger towel by making the background strips longer and adding more whales – your whole family could have matching towels, all in different colours.

instructions

2

Transfer the templates for the whales and water spurts to the webbing: place the webbing over a template, paper side up, and trace the lines of the template. Cut out the shape roughly. The towel features seven whales at each end (one set facing to the left and one set facing to the right), but you may need more or fewer whales depending on the size of your towel.

3

Place each shape, paper side up, on the wrong side of the appropriate fabric. Iron for 3–4 seconds (no steam). Cut out the shapes accurately.

1

Take the fabric for the sea and draw two rectangles side by side, with a small gap between them, using the fabric marker. Make each rectangle the width of the towel x 7cm (2¾in).

4

Peel off the backing paper and arrange the whales, coated side down, on the right side of the sea background (use the photo for guidance on positioning). Position a spurt of water over each whale's head, tucking it slightly under the head. Iron in place and leave the motifs to cool (see page 107).

Place a piece of webbing, paper side up, on the wrong side of each sea background piece. Iron for 3–4 seconds (no steam) and then leave to cool. Peel off the backing paper.

Using the freehand foot, machine-stitch carefully around each motif just inside the edge.

Backstitch the whales' facial features using three strands of black embroidery thread, and make French knots for the eyes. (For details of how to work the hand stitches, see pages 108–11.) If you prefer to have a drawn line to follow, use an erasable fabric marker or an iron-on transfer pen (see page 107).

Embroider splashes around the spurts, using three strands of blue embroidery thread and working a few stitches over each other to make the shapes.

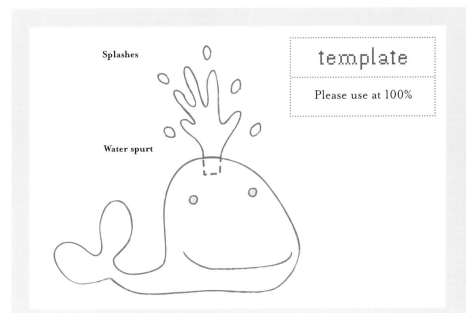

Splashes

Water spurt

template

Please use at 100%

Cut out each sea background: it should measure the width of the towel x 7cm (2¾in).

Position each strip of whales at each end of the towel. The base of the whales should face the edge of the towel. Iron in place and leave to cool (see page 107).

9

Machine-stitch around each strip using a zigzag foot. The towel is ready to make bathtime fun!

teddy hat

Fleece fabric: 0.5m x 147cm
(½yd x 58in)

Scraps of patterned cotton
fabric (inner ears and muzzle)

Double-sided fusible webbing
(such as Bondaweb) (muzzle)

Embroidery thread (black and
yellow, or colours to suit)

Embroidery needle

Sewing machine

Sewing thread

Erasable marker and iron-on
transfer pen

This hat is practical as well as very cute. It will keep baby's head warm when out and about, and makes fun at-home loungewear! It will make a great present for a new baby, and the neutral colours mean it's suitable for a boy or a girl.

instructions

3

Place the outer and inner ear with right sides together, pin and tack. Machine-stitch around each ear with a 6mm ($^1/_4$in) seam, leaving the base open. Cut triangular notches out of the seam allowance to reduce bulk. Turn the ears right side out and press with your fingers.

4

Lay one hat piece with right side uppermost. With raw edge to raw edge, position each ear as marked on the template, the ear lying on the hat. Pin and tack.

Place the two hat pieces with right sides together. Machine-stitch around the hat with a 6mm ($^1/_4$in) seam, sewing in the ears and leaving the base open.

1

Use the templates to cut out the hat pieces, outer ears and band from the fleece, and inner ears from the cotton fabric. The pieces should include a seam allowance of 6mm ($^1/_4$in).

Use an erasable fabric marker to mark the positions of the ears (see pages 106–7).

2

Make the muzzle: place the webbing over the template, paper side up, and trace the lines. Cut out the shape roughly; place paper side up on the wrong side of the cotton fabric. Iron for 3–4 seconds (no steam). Cut out the muzzle accurately. Remove the backing paper.

5

Hem one long edge of the band. With right sides together, stitch the short ends with a 6mm ($^1/_4$in) seam. Press the seam open with your fingers. Pin the raw edge of the band to the base of the hat, right side of band to wrong side of hat. Make sure that the band's seam is at the back of the hat (inner ears are on the front of the hat). Tack and machine-stitch in place.

Use the iron-on transfer pen to transfer the nose and mouth to the muzzle. Using six strands of black embroidery thread, backstitch the line under the nose and along the mouth. (For details of how to work the hand stitches, see pages 108–11.) Embroider the nose using satin stitch.

Whipstitch the muzzle to the hat using three strands of embroidery thread. Make small stitches with a fairly small space between each one. (The motif is not ironed into position, as the heat would flatten the surrounding fleece.)

Using six strands of black embroidery thread, backstitch a circle for each eye and then fill it in using two layers of satin stitch to give a raised effect.

Fold the band to the right side of the hat to create the turn-up.

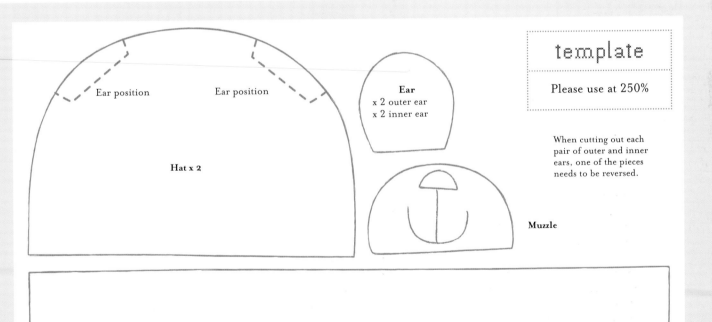

Ear position   Ear position

Hat x 2

Ear
x 2 outer ear
x 2 inner ear

template

Please use at 250%

When cutting out each pair of outer and inner ears, one of the pieces needs to be reversed.

Muzzle

Band

rabbit blankie

Soft fabric, such as brushed cotton winceyette or towelling, in white or cream: 0.5m x 114/147cm ($^{1}/_{2}$yd x 45/58in) (body and inner ears)

Patterned cotton fabric: 0.5m x 114cm ($^{1}/_{2}$yd x 45in) (head, ears, tail and paws)

Double-sided fusible webbing (such as Bondaweb) (paws, tail, inner ears)

Embroidery thread (black and a colour)

Embroidery needle

Sewing machine

Sewing thread

Erasable fabric marker or iron-on transfer pen (optional)

Toy stuffing

This gorgeous rabbit comforter blanket is going to be well loved. It is perfect for a baby, as the soft body is cosy and warm; when baby is a little older, the head is ideal for tiny hands to grip. Toddlers will adore it too. Make it as a gift for a new baby and choose fabric colours according to whether the new arrival is a girl or a boy!

instructions

Make the blankie in a neutral colour, or in a traditional pale blue for a boy or pink for a girl. Use a soft fabric such as winceyette or fleece for the body, to make the comforter cosy.

Sew the two pieces for the back of the head, right sides together, along the centre back with a 6mm (¼in) seam.

With right sides together, place the front and back head pieces on top of each other. Machine-stitch around the head with a 6mm (¼in) seam, sewing in the ears and leaving the neck edge open. You may find it easier to sew in the ears by hand, using backstitch, because the stuffing may make the head too bulky to go under the machine's foot. Turn the head right side out.

If you wish, use an erasable fabric marker or iron-on transfer pen to mark the facial features on the head. Using six strands of black embroidery thread, stitch the nose and mouth using backstitch. Embroider the eyes using satin stitch. Stuff the head firmly. Make sure there is stuffing right up to the bottom end of the neck, or the head will flop rather than standing up.

Lay the front of the body with the right side uppermost. Lay the head on top, the back of the head uppermost, with the base of the neck to the edge of the body and the head extending into the body area. Pin and tack.

Place the front and back of the body with right sides together, and pin and tack. Machine-stitch all the way around the body, catching in the head, and leaving a gap along the bottom edge for turning. Again, you may find it easier to sew in the head by hand, using backstitch, because the stuffing may make the neck too bulky to go under the machine foot.

Turn the rabbit right side out, pushing out all his paws carefully. Slipstitch the gap to close it. Your little rabbit is ready to be loved!

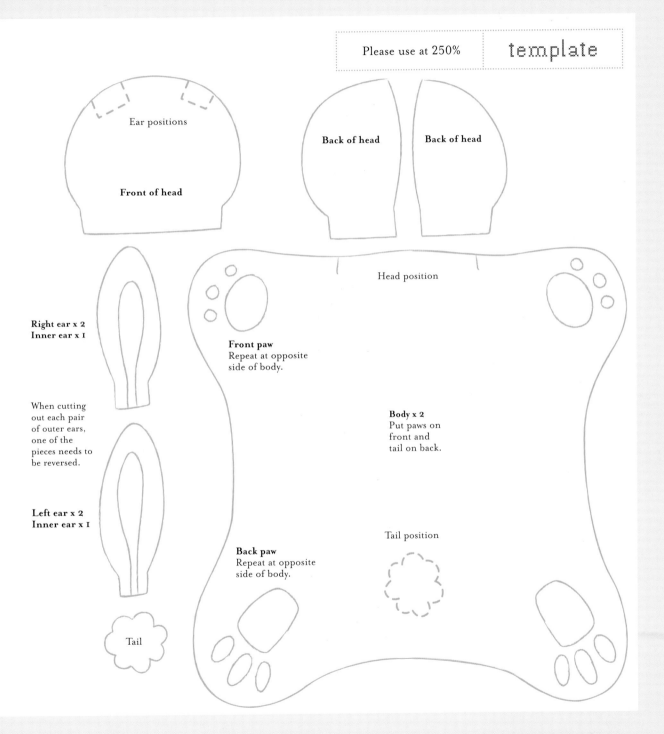

Please use at 250%

template

Ear positions

Front of head

Back of head

Back of head

Head position

Right ear x 2
Inner ear x 1

Front paw
Repeat at opposite
side of body.

Body x 2
Put paws on
front and
tail on back.

When cutting
out each pair
of outer ears,
one of the
pieces needs to
be reversed.

Left ear x 2
Inner ear x 1

Tail position

Back paw
Repeat at opposite
side of body.

Tail

monster play mat

Thick plain fabric, such as corduroy:
125cm x 114cm (1½yd x 45in)
(surface of mat)

Patterned or plain fabric:
125cm x 114cm (1½yd x 45in)
(back of mat)

Scraps of patterned cotton fabrics
(bodies, legs, feelers and nostrils)

Scraps of yellow patterned fabrics,
preferably with different textures
(stars)

Double-sided fusible webbing (such
as Bondaweb) (monsters
and stars)

Embroidery thread (black)

Embroidery needle

Thick wadding: 1m (1⅛yd) square

Sewing machine with a zigzag foot
and a freehand foot

Sewing thread

Erasable fabric marker
or iron-on transfer pen (optional)

Toy stuffing

Little monsters will love playing on this mat: there are plenty of textures and colours to keep them interested. It is also perfect for a baby who is just learning to sit up, or for a slightly older child to lie on and look at a book or take a nap.

instructions

Add dried beans or gravel to make him heavier, but sew in a lining if you use gravel.

allowance, leaving a gap in the straight side for turning. Turn right side out. Turn the open edges to the inside and slipstitch to close.

Position the ears on the dog, using the photo for guidance, and sew on firmly. Use a double thickness of thread and whipstitch. Secure the thread to the body under the ears to start, and finish the stitching under the ear, close to the top, so the stitches will be hidden.

Make the tail and legs. Place the pieces with right sides together and machine-stitch around the edges with a 6mm ($\frac{1}{4}$in) seam, leaving the end that attaches to the body open. Turn right side out and stuff quite firmly.

10

Whipstitch the legs to the body, turning in 6mm ($\frac{1}{4}$in) at the top of the leg. Sew right around the edges, forming a circle. Secure the thread to the body under the leg to start, and finish

the stitching just under the top of the leg. Repeat the procedure to attach the tail.

Embroider the facial features. Use backstitch for a smiling mouth and satin stitch for the eyes. Sew an eye, go down to the mouth with the same piece of thread and then go back to do the other eye.

This little sausage dog is now ready to guard the nursery door, keeping draughts out and the heat in.

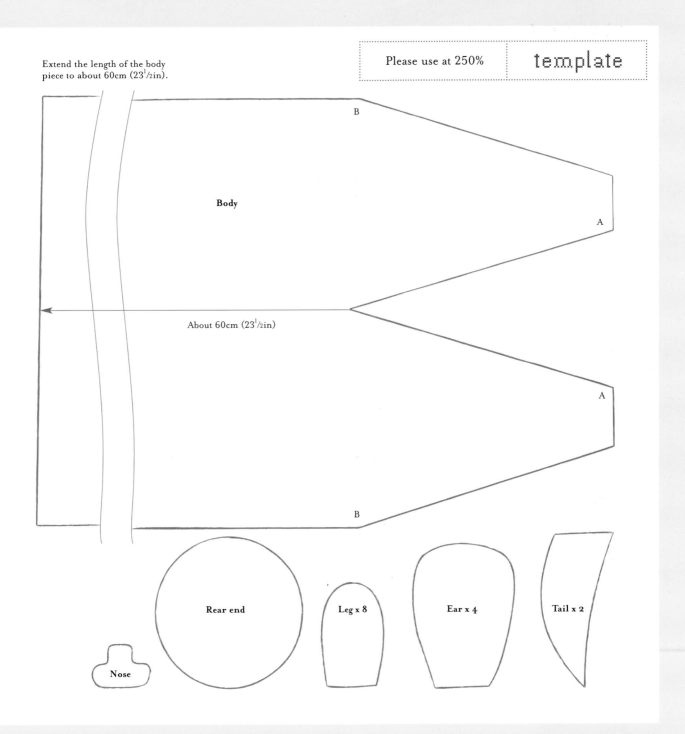

Extend the length of the body piece to about 60cm (23$\frac{1}{2}$in).

Please use at 250%

template

Body

B

A

← About 60cm (23$\frac{1}{2}$in)

A

B

Nose

Rear end

Leg x 8

Ear x 4

Tail x 2

instructions

Cut a square of soft fabric for the cushion front, 69 x 69cm (27 x 27in).

Make the borders and corner squares. Cut the webbing: four rectangles, 69 x 6.5cm (27 x 2½in), and four squares, 6.5 x 6.5cm (2½ x 2½in). Fix the webbing to the fabric: place it, paper side up, on the wrong side of the fabric. Iron for 3–4 seconds (no steam).

Cut out the shapes, peel off the backing paper and lay them, coated side down, on the right side of the front of the cushion. Iron in place and leave to cool (see pages 106–7).

Machine-stitch around the edges of the corner square/border pieces using a zigzag stitch (not the outer edge: it will be caught in the cushion's seam).

Make the pig. Transfer the templates to the webbing: place the webbing over the template, paper side up, and trace the lines of the template. Cut out the shape roughly. Place each shape, paper side up, on the wrong side of the appropriate fabric. Iron for 3–4 seconds (no steam). Cut out the shapes accurately.

Peel off the backing paper and lay the pieces, coated side down, on the front of the cushion. Tuck the ends of the back legs, ears and tail behind the main body piece. Iron in place and leave to cool.

Sew blanket stitch around the edge of each piece, using six strands of embroidery thread. (For details of how to work the hand stitches, see pages 108–11.)

Sew on the facial features, using six strands of black embroidery thread. Use satin stitch for the eyes and backstitch for the mouth. If you prefer to have a drawn line to follow, use an erasable fabric marker or iron-on transfer pen (see page 107).

Using six strands of embroidery thread, backstitch a cross for a tummy button and two crosses for nostrils.

Make the back of the cushion. Cut two rectangles of the soft fabric, measuring 69 x 42cm (27 x 16½in). On each piece, fold over 4cm (1½in) on the long edge to the wrong side, tuck the raw edge under and hem.

Place the back and front of the cushion with right sides together, with the hemmed edges of the back facing towards the centre of the cushion (these pieces overlap). Pin around all four edges, tack and then sew with a 1.5cm (½in) seam. Reinforce the corners by stitching over them again with a small stitch. Trim the seam and trim across the corners.

Turn the cushion cover the right side out, then slip the cushion pad through the back opening.

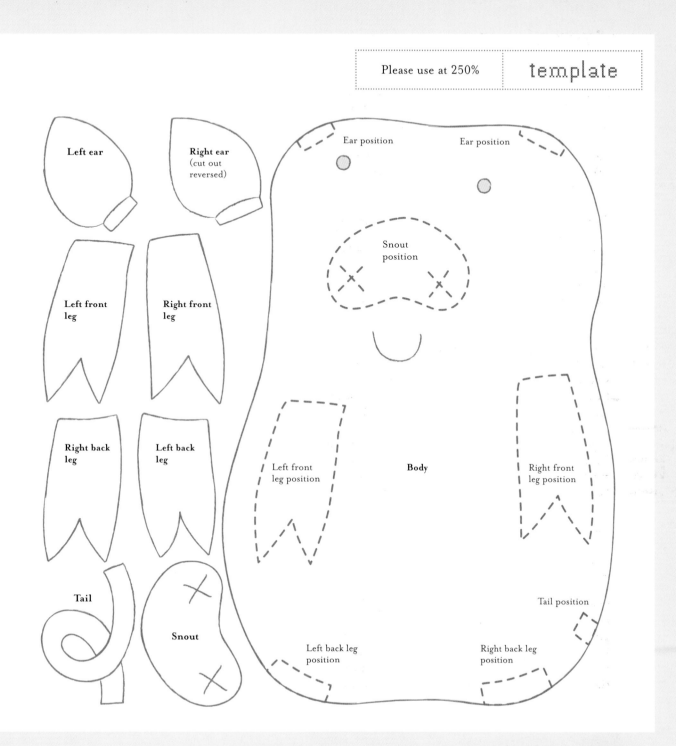

Left ear

Right ear
(cut out
reversed)

Left front
leg

Right front
leg

Right back
leg

Left back
leg

Tail

Snout

Ear position   Ear position

Snout
position

Left front
leg position

Body

Right front
leg position

Left back leg
position

Tail position

Right back leg
position

henry the pig

Corduroy fabric in a bright colour: 0.25m x 114cm (¹/₄yd x 45in) (body and snout)

Scraps of striped cotton fabric (legs)

Scraps of patterned cotton fabric (ears and tail)

Double-sided fusible webbing (such as Bondaweb) (tail)

Embroidery thread (black, red and blue, or colours to suit)

Embroidery needle

Sewing machine

Sewing thread

Erasable fabric marker or iron-on transfer pen

Toy stuffing

Henry is a charming pig: he is loyal, friendly and very cute! He is very huggable, too, and his corduroy body gives him an interesting texture. You could make a pair of porkers – change Henry into Henrietta by using a paler corduroy and a more subtle striped material for the limbs.

instructions

Use the templates to cut out the pattern pieces (see page 106): the body pieces in corduroy, the legs in striped fabric and the ears and tail in patterned fabric. Use a fabric marker to transfer pattern markings such as the ear positions (see page 107.)

Make the ears. Backstitch the line of the inner ear on the front ear piece using six strands of embroidery thread. (For details of how to work the hand stitches, see pages 108–11.) Place the front and back of the ear with wrong sides together. Sew around the edge in blanket stitch, leaving the bottom open. Stuff the ears (you need to make sure there is stuffing right up to the bottom end of each ear, or it will flop rather than stand up).

Make the legs. Place the two back pieces with right sides together and machine-stitch along the back of the leg (the long, slightly curved edge) with a 6mm (¹/₄in) seam.

Take the front leg piece and place it on the back piece, right sides together. Sew around the edge with a 6mm (¹/₄in) seam, leaving the top of the leg open. Turn right side out, using a pencil to gently push out the points. Stuff firmly.

Transfer the template for the tail to the webbing: place the webbing over the template, paper side up, and trace the lines of the template. Cut out the shape roughly. Place the shape, paper side up, on the wrong side of the fabric. Iron for 3–4 seconds (no steam).

Cut out the shape accurately. Peel off the backing paper and lay it, coated side down, on the wrong side of the fabric. Iron in place and leave to cool (see page 107). Cut out the double-sided tail. Sew around the shape with blanket stitch, as for the ears.

Attach the legs and ears to the front body piece. Lay them on the right side of the body in the marked positions, with raw edges together and the limbs and ears lying on the body (the back of each is uppermost, so everything faces the correct way when the pig is finished). Pin and tack in place. Make sure that the tops of the ears and limbs extend slightly above the body piece, so they will be caught securely in the seam.

Make up the back body piece: place the two sections with right sides together and machine-stitch along the pig's backbone with a 6mm (¹/₄in) seam.

Take the gusset piece for the pig's rear end and pin at the bottom of the front body, with right sides together, so the centre lies in the middle of the space between his legs. Tack.

instructions

The snout is a little tricky: remember to make the whipstitches close together when you attach it to the body, so the stuffing doesn't poke out.

 9

Place the back and front body with right sides together, then pin round as far as the gusset and tack. Machine-stitch around the body as far as each side of the gusset with a 6mm ($\frac{1}{4}$in) seam. Continue stitching from the top of the gusset around the front body piece, trapping in the legs. Sew around the back gusset, leaving a gap in the middle for turning.

 10

Turn the pig right side out. Sew a cross for a tummy button, using six strands of embroidery thread. Stuff the body.

 11

Make the snout. Take the long strip and fold with right sides together. Machine-stitch the narrow end with a 6mm ($\frac{1}{4}$in) seam. Press the seam open with your fingers. With right sides together, pin on the front of the snout, with the dip in the snout over the join. Tack all the way round, making sure it all matches well, then machine-stitch with a 6mm ($\frac{1}{4}$in) seam. (If you prefer, you can sew the snout together by hand.)

 12

Stuff the snout lightly. Embroider on two crosses with six strands of embroidery thread for the nostrils. Position the snout on the face. Slipstitch around the edge to attach it,

turning under 6mm ($\frac{1}{4}$in). Before you complete the sewing, stuff the snout more firmly.

 13

Embroider the facial features using three strands of black embroidery thread. For the eyes, backstitch a small circle and then fill it with satin stitch. Sew two layers to make the eyes slightly raised. Backstitch the mouth using the photo to guide you.

 14

Slipstitch the gap in the pig's rear end to close it (when you reach the middle of the gap, tuck in the tip of the tail and sew it into position).

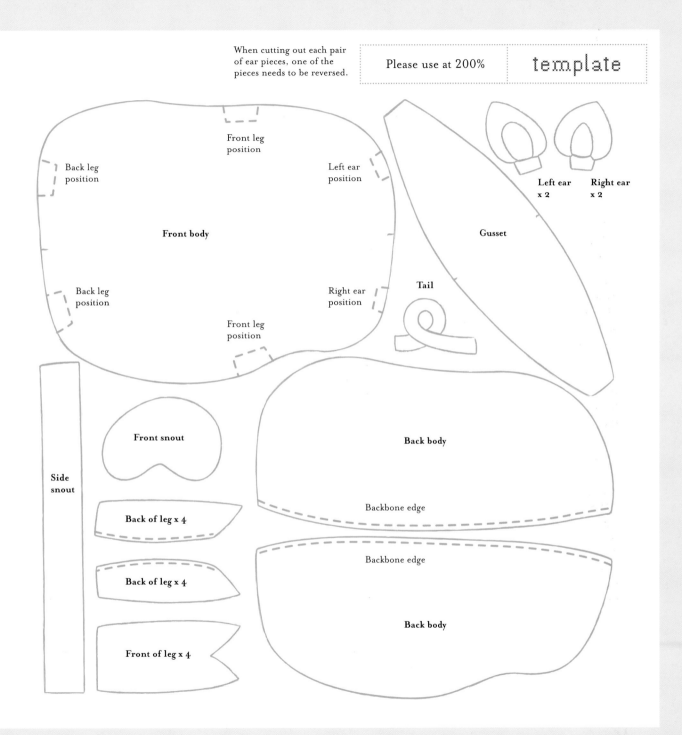

When cutting out each pair
of ear pieces, one of the
pieces needs to be reversed.

Please use at 200%

template

Back leg
position

Front leg
position

Left ear
position

Front body

Left ear
x 2

Right ear
x 2

Gusset

Back leg
position

Right ear
position

Tail

Front leg
position

Side
snout

Front snout

Back body

Backbone edge

Back of leg x 4

Backbone edge

Back of leg x 4

Front of leg x 4

Back body

sleepy ted mobile

The sleepy teddies and moon and stars dangling from this mobile contain a lot of small stitches and intricate detail, so if you love sewing, it will be perfect for you. The mobile is bound to become a treasured keepsake.

instructions

If you have a specific nursery theme, make a mobile to match, using the techniques for this project.

9

Take one teddy and ribbon and wrap the ribbon around the hoop, as in the photo, making sure the teddy will face outwards. Secure the ribbon to the hoop with a little stitch just inside the rim, leaving a long tail for tying with all the other ribbons above the hoop.

Do this with the other teddies and stars, alternating them at equal intervals around the edge, each hanging at a slightly different depth.

10

Hold the mobile by the ribbons and make sure it hangs straight. Add the moon's ribbon to the bundle, then knot all the ribbons together. You may need to adjust it so that the ring is level. Tie the loose ends into a bow or another knot, so the mobile can be suspended from a hook. The mobile is now ready to hang in the nursery – perfect for helping a little person to get to sleep!

In each pair of pieces for the teddy, moon, stars, hat and inner ears, one of the pieces is reversed.

Please use at 100%

template

Hat x 6

Moon x 2

Teddy x 6

Tummy x 6

Star x 6

Details for 'asleep' face

Details for 'awake' face

Cut muzzle as separate piece.

Cut muzzle as separate piece.

toy tidy

You will need

Striped cotton fabric:
2m x 114cm (2¼yd x 45in)
(front, back and handles)

Corduroy fabric: 1m x 114cm
(1⅛yd x 45in) (pockets)

Scraps of patterned cotton
fabric (animals)

Double-sided fusible webbing
(such as Bondaweb)

Embroidery thread (black)

Embroidery needle

Sewing machine with
a freehand foot and
a zigzag foot

Sewing thread

Metre ruler and set square

Erasable fabric marker

Iron-on transfer pen
(optional)

A toy tidy will encourage toddlers to put away their toys without too much fuss! The cord pockets are durable, so lots of things can be stuffed inside. Hang this tidy from a dado rail, or set two small hooks in the perfect place on the wall.

instructions

6

7

10

If you want a bigger tidy, make the main pieces bigger and add more pockets, repeating the animals.

Cut the front and back from striped fabric, with the stripes running vertically. Make each piece 83 x 63cm (33 x 25in).

Cut the pieces for the six pockets out of the corduroy: you need twelve rectangles, 23 x 25cm (9 x 10in).

Make the animals. Transfer the templates to the webbing: place the webbing over a template, paper side up, and trace the lines of the template. Cut out the shapes roughly. Place each shape, paper side up, on the wrong side of the appropriate fabric. For the sheep's head and legs, and the rabbit's and cat's inner ears, use a fabric that contrasts with the body. Iron for 3–4 seconds (no steam). Cut out the shapes accurately.

Peel off the backing paper from the animals and arrange the bodies, coated side down, on the right side of six of the pocket pieces (long sides are top and bottom). Iron in place and leave to cool (see page 107). Attach other parts such as the sheep's face and legs (tuck under the body), and details such as inner ears, in the same way.

Using the freehand foot, machine-stitch around each animal, just inside the edge, using a straight stitch. Repeat to highlight other features on the animals, as shown in the photos. A thread in a contrasting colour looks good. You can hand-stitch these pieces if you prefer.

Create the animals' faces. If you wish, use an erasable fabric marker or iron-on transfer pen to mark the facial features on each creature.

Using six strands of black embroidery thread, stitch the mouths using backstitch, make French knots for the eyes (satin stitch for the eyes on the rabbit and pig), and satin stitch for the noses on the dog and cat. For nostrils, use cross-stitch on the pig and backstitch on the sheep. (For details of how to work the hand stitches, see pages 108–11.)

Place the back and front of each pocket with right sides together, and pin and tack. Machine-stitch around the edges with a 1.5cm (½in) seam, leaving a small gap along the bottom for turning right side out.

ella the mouse

Scraps of patterned cotton fabric (body)

Scraps of patterned cotton fabric (ears, legs, tail, nose)

Double-sided fusible webbing (such as Bondaweb) (legs, nose and tail)

Embroidery thread (black and yellow, or colour to suit)

Embroidery needle

Sewing machine with a freehand foot

Sewing thread

Erasable fabric marker

Toy stuffing

Ella is quite a shy mouse, but she will be a good friend to any little person who loves her. Ella has lovely beady eyes; if you are making her for an older child, you could use real beads, but make sure you sew them on very securely.

olivia the sheep

Olivia is a lively sheep and can't wait to get up to mischief with her new owner! She is bound to be a hit: her soft, round body is very cuddly and her little legs give her a slightly comic appearance.

lucy
the elephant

Scraps of patterned cotton fabric (body/head/trunk)

Scraps of patterned cotton fabric (ears and legs)

Embroidery thread (black, red, blue and pink, or colours to suit)

Embroidery needle

Sewing machine

Sewing thread

Erasable fabric marker

Toy stuffing

Lucy is one of the trickier animals to make, due to her long trunk. I have used a very busy body fabric and a much simpler pattern for the legs and ears. You could try doing the opposite – it will produce a completely different effect.

instructions

Use the templates to make a pattern and cut out the pieces for the elephant. Use a fabric marker to transfer pattern markings to the pieces (see pages 106–7).

Make the legs. Fold each piece in half, right sides together. Pin and tack along the long edge, then machine-stitch with a 6mm (¼in) seam. Turn right side out. Slipstitch the base of the foot to the bottom of the leg, turning in 6mm (¼in) as you go. (For details of how to work the hand stitches, see pages 108–11.) Stuff quite firmly.

Embroider the toes at the bottom of each leg, using six strands of embroidery thread and backstitch.

Make the body by placing the sections with right sides together, pinning, tacking and machine-stitching with a 6mm (¼in) seam. Start by attaching the backbone/upper trunk section to the two side panels. Sew along the backbone and down the trunk; sew the underside of the trunk.

Lay the legs on the right side of the side panels as marked, with raw edges together and the legs lying on the body. The back seam of the legs should be facing the back of the body. Pin and tack in place. Make sure that the tops of the legs extend slightly above the body piece, to ensure that they will be caught securely in the seam.

Take the belly piece and pin and tack into position.

Machine-stitch around the belly gusset with a 6mm (¼in) seam, leaving it open where the belly gusset meets the backbone/ trunk section at the elephant's rear end; the bottom end of the trunk is also left open. The area just under her trunk can be tricky to machine, but if a tiny gap remains, you can always slipstitch the edges together.

Turn the body the right way out and stuff through the rear end. Use a pencil to get the stuffing right down the trunk. Sew on the end of the trunk, using the same method as for the feet; before doing this, embroider two nostrils on the end piece – use three strands of embroidery thread and sew two little lines side by side for each nostril.

Place the two pieces for each ear with wrong sides together. Pin and tack. Embroider all the way around the edge of each ear with three strands of embroidery thread, using blanket stitch, and stuffing them lightly before finishing the row of stitching.

Position the ears on the head and attach with slipstitch, using three strands of embroidery thread and working through the blanket stitch.

instructions

8

Embroider the facial features using six strands of black embroidery thread. For the eyes, make French knots. Backstitch a mouth under the trunk.

9

Make the tail by cutting six strands of embroidery thread, about 20cm (8in) long, in different colours. Tie a knot in one end and then thread all six strands through a large-eyed needle and push it through the rear end of the elephant (from inside the body) where the tail is to go. Plait the tail to the required length, knot the end and trim off the excess.

10

Slipstitch the gap in the rear end to close it, adding more stuffing to the elephant first if necessary.

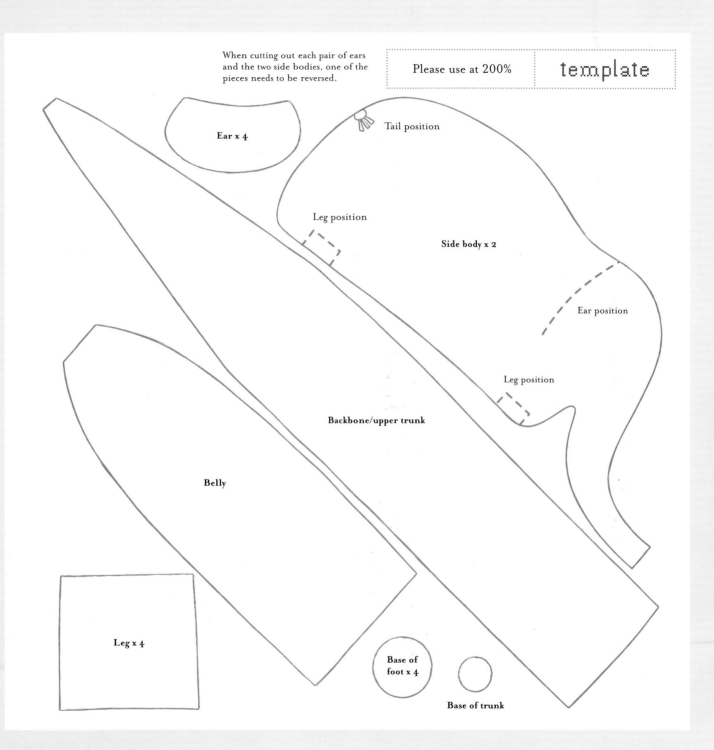

When cutting out each pair of ears
and the two side bodies, one of the
pieces needs to be reversed.

Please use at 200% | template

Ear x 4

Tail position

Leg position

Side body x 2

Ear position

Leg position

Backbone/upper trunk

Belly

Leg x 4

Base of
foot x 4

Base of trunk

Using a sewing machine

You will need a sewing machine for basic operations such as seaming together pattern pieces, and to create decorative stitching.

Free-motion sewing

For lots of the projects, you will need a freehand foot to allow you to do free-motion sewing. This spring-loaded foot 'hops', allowing you to manoeuvre the fabric easily to stitch curves and other shapes. You can purchase one from a haberdashery department or a sewing machine shop. Check in the store to find out which foot will fit on your sewing machine.

Free-motion stitch is rather like drawing with a sewing machine, and is very simple once you get the hang of it. You may need to practise before sewing something tiny. Part of the charm of free-motion stitching is that you can create lines that look quite naive yet are still very skilful and effective. For some pieces you may find it easier to use an embroidery hoop to hold the fabric. It will give you more control and prevent the fabric from being dragged down into the machine. It will also make it safer for you and ensure that you don't get your hand caught by the needle.

Stitching around a motif

1 Attach the foot and lower the feed dogs on the machine (these help drag fabric through the machine, which you don't want when you're doing free-motion sewing).

2 Stitch around the motifs, a little way in from the edge, at whatever speed you like. The key to producing a neat effect is to move the fabric round slowly but have the needle working at a fast pace.

3 To start and finish stitching, just go back and forth over the stitching line a couple of times. Alternatively, leave some thread hanging from both ends and finish it off by hand afterwards.

Seams

The seam allowances included in most of the project templates are 6mm ($^1/_4$in), but if you prefer to have a larger seam to give you extra room when sewing, you can add extra around the template as you cut it out. (For larger pieces of fabric, there are seam allowances of 1.5cm [$^1/_2$in].) Stitch the seam, press it and then trim it to 6mm ($^1/_4$in).

To ensure that a curved seam lies flat when the item is turned right side out, cut little triangular notches of fabric out of the seam allowance.

Acknowledgments

I have many people to thank for the completion of my book. First, I would like to thank everyone at Anova Books for making this book possible and for all their help along the way. A special thanks to Miriam, Nihal, Fiona, and Louise and also to Christina for the wonderful photographs. I would also like to thank my family for their constant support and for believing in me. A big thanks also goes to my friends for their great interest and encouragement in everything I do. Finally, I would like to thank Coats Crafts UK for providing a lot of the fabrics and threads I used in the projects and also for giving me the experience at designing and writing craft projects.

The publisher would like to thank our models Valerio Thompson and Lara Yun Moeller.

Photography by Christina Wilson.